The Emperor and the Nightingale

Level 4

Retold by Marie Crook

Series Editors: Annie Hughes and Melanie Williams

Pearson Education Limited
Edinburgh Gate, Harlow
Essex CM20 2JE, England
and Associated Companies throughout the world.

ISBN 0582 344042

First published by Librairie du Liban Publishers, 1996
This adaptation first published 2000 under licence by
Penguin Books
© 2000 Penguin Books Ltd
Illustrations © 1996 Librairie du Liban

1 3 5 7 9 10 8 6 4 2

Illustrations by Angus McBride
Design by Traffika Publishing/Wendi Watson

All rights reserved; no part of this publication may be reproduced, stored in a retrieval system, or transmitted in any form or by any means, electronic, mechanical, photocopying, recording, or otherwise, without the prior written permission of the Publishers.

Printed in Scotland by Scotprint, Musselburgh

Published by Pearson Education Limited in association with Penguin Books Ltd, both companies being subsidiaries of Pearson Plc

---

For a complete list of the titles available in the Penguin Young Readers series please write to your local Pearson Education office or to:
Marketing Department, Penguin Longman Publishing,
5 Bentinck Street, London W1M 5RN

Once upon a time in China, there was an old and powerful Emperor. He lived in an enormous palace by a deep lake. The Emperor loved his palace and his beautiful gardens, but there was one problem. It was too quiet! And this Emperor hated peace and quiet!

'I want music!' he used to cry, 'every morning, every afternoon, every evening, and every night! Music!'

And the Emperor always got what he wanted.

So everywhere he went, he was surrounded by music. But the music was so loud that the Emperor did not hear the sweetest song of all.

The Emperor and his musical palace were very famous. Hundreds of people came every week to smell the flowers in the Emperor's garden, to sit beside the deep lake, and to listen to the sound of the Emperor's music echoing through the palace. It was such a strange and beautiful place, that great authors came from far away countries to write poems and books about it.

One day, the Emperor received one of these books. He sat all day in his golden chair, reading about his fine clothes, his expensive jewellery, and his beautiful nightingale.

'My beautiful nightingale? What beautiful nightingale?' cried the Emperor, 'I don't know anything about a nightingale!'

The author had written hundreds of pages about the Emperor's musical palace.

'...But the sweetest sound of all,' he wrote, 'is the song of the nightingale.'

The Emperor was a little cross and confused; he read on, more and more quickly.

'The Emperor is truly a lucky man to own such a talented creature. While he, himself, is a very rich man, it is surely the nightingale which is the greatest treasure of all.'

'A lucky man?' cried the Emperor. 'A lucky man? The nightingale is my greatest treasure and I, the Emperor of China, the great and powerful Emperor, have never even heard its song!'

'Bring me the nightingale now!' he shouted. 'If the nightingale is not in my palace by this evening, you'll all be sorry!'

The Emperor's men were very frightened, because they had not seen a nightingale either nor ever heard its song.

'Don't worry, your Majesty,' one of the men said, 'we'll find the nightingale. You'll hear its song this evening.'

The Emperor's men quickly raced out of the room. Then they stopped and looked at each other.

'What are we going to do now?' they cried.

'I know,' said one of the men, 'let's ask everyone in the palace. There must be someone who's heard the nightingale's song.'

They asked everybody in the Emperor's enormous palace and nobody had ever seen or heard the nightingale.

'The only thing we ever hear,' they said, 'is the Emperor's music, echoing through the palace.'

Finally, they found a little kitchen girl who had heard the nightingale's song.

'Follow me!' she said.

The Emperor's men followed the little kitchen girl out of the palace and into the garden.

They listened very carefully for the nightingale's song, but the men had never been out of the palace before and they had no idea what a nightingale sounded like.

Suddenly, they heard a noise, swish, swish.

'Aha!' cried the men, 'that must be the nightingale!'

'Don't be silly,' laughed the kitchen girl, 'that's just the sound of the wind in the trees!'

Then they heard a deep sound, moooooo.

'What a strange and beautiful song,' said one of the men, 'it must be the nightingale!'

'Oh, you are funny,' laughed the kitchen girl, 'have you never heard a cow before?'

'Of course we have,' said the men quickly.

They walked a little further down the path.

'Listen!' cried one of the men, 'I can definitely hear it now!'

'That's not the nightingale,' smiled the kitchen girl, 'that's only a little frog. Look at it!'

'Of course, of course,' said the men, but they were a little worried because they did not know what a nightingale looked like and they did not know what a nightingale sounded like.

They asked the little kitchen girl, but she just smiled and said, 'wait and see.'

So the men tried to imagine what the nightingale would look like.

'It must be very big,' said one of the men, 'because its voice is so loud.'

'Yes,' said another, 'and it must be as green as the forest because it is so difficult to see among the trees.'

'And its voice is so beautiful,' the last man said, 'so it must be beautiful too. I imagine that the nightingale will be as big as a cow, and as beautiful as a butterfly...

...It'll have golden feathers and a silver tail.'

Suddenly the little kitchen girl cried, 'Stop!'
The Emperor's men were talking so much that they did not hear the nightingale's song.

'Listen!' she said.

So they listened, and it was the most beautiful song they had ever heard. But when they looked up, they could only see a little bird with brown feathers.

'This,' smiled the little kitchen girl, 'is the nightingale.'

'O, Nightingale!' they said, 'we would be very grateful if you would come to the palace this evening. The Emperor will be waiting for you in the great hall.'

Back at the palace, the Emperor was preparing the great hall. When he heard the nightingale had agreed to come, he was very excited.

'Clean this room from the floor to the ceiling!' he shouted. So the floor was cleaned and the walls were washed, until everything was perfect.

'Now do it again!' cried the Emperor.

So they cleaned everything again, but the Emperor was still not happy.

'Bring me one thousand lanterns!' he said. So his men brought one thousand lanterns.

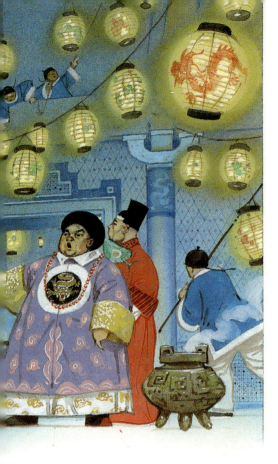

'For my special guest,' he said, 'I want a beautiful golden perch.'

'This must be the best festival we've ever had!' he cried. 'It must be perfect!'

The Emperor was very nervous, and when he was nervous, he was very fussy, very bossy, and very angry. The men were afraid of the Emperor when he was angry, so they worked hard.

Finally, everything was ready. The Emperor looked around the great hall very slowly and very carefully. The men waited for a response.

Then the Emperor spoke.

'Perfect!' he said, 'let the festival begin!'

The great hall was very quiet while everyone waited for the nightingale to arrive.

Suddenly, it flew in through the window and sat on its golden perch.

'You may sing for us, little bird,' said the Emperor. And the nightingale sang its finest song for the Emperor and his guests.

Its voice was as sweet as sugar though its song was a strange song because it was both happy and sad, both gentle and powerful.

The Emperor's guests were delighted. They had never heard such a beautiful song. The Emperor was so happy that he had tears in his eyes.

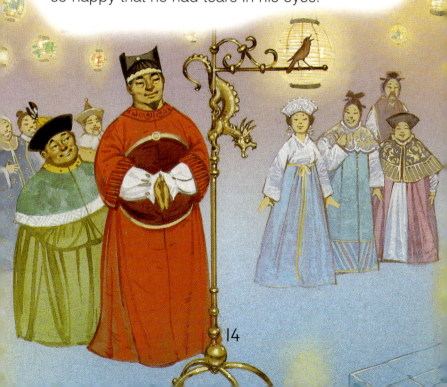

When the nightingale finished, there was silence. Then the Emperor spoke.

'Oh, thank you,' he said, 'that was the most beautiful song I've ever heard. I'd like to give you something in return. What would you like?' he asked the nightingale, 'you may have anything you wish.'

'Your Majesty,' replied the nightingale, 'I am so glad that my song made you happy. Please do not give me anything. To bring smiles to everyone's faces is enough.'

'Then, please,' said the Emperor, 'let me give you a home. Come and live with me in the palace. You can have this golden cage and you can sing all day.'

'But the trees and the forest are my home,' said the little nightingale.

'My song is much more beautiful in the forest because I am happy there.'

The Emperor was too excited to listen to the nightingale. So the nightingale lived in the palace with the Emperor and it sang every day.

However, the nightingale soon got bored. Its golden perch was hard and uncomfortable, and it wanted to fly through the forest, perch on the trees and sleep in its soft nest.

After two weeks in its golden cage, the nightingale started to feel very sad.

One day, the nightingale said to the Emperor, 'Your Majesty, I am lonely. Please allow me to go outside. I need to fly through the sky, to sit in the trees, and to see the other animals in the forest.'

The Emperor allowed the nightingale to visit the forest every morning. But the nightingale was his greatest treasure and he did not want to lose it. He put golden strings on the nightingale's little feet and when it flew outside, the Emperor's men held the strings so that it could not fly away.

Every evening, the nightingale sat in its golden cage and sang to the Emperor. Each time, the Emperor had tears in his eyes, and each time, he told the little bird,

'You are my greatest treasure!'

Then, one day, a big box arrived at the palace. It was a gift from the Emperor of Japan. There was a note on the box which said,

'I've heard about your lovely nightingale. Here is another bird for you. Can you decide which is the most valuable?'

The Emperor was very excited. 'What a mystery!' he cried, 'let's open it!'

Inside the box, there was a beautiful, golden bird on a heavy golden perch. It had diamonds instead of eyes and beautiful jewels instead of wings.
The Emperor was delighted. 'It's the most fantastic thing I've ever seen,' he cried.

'If it could sing, it'd be as valuable as my nightingale,' he said, 'but it's a golden bird, and golden birds can't sing.'
'Excuse me, your Majesty,' said the Emperor's watchmaker, who had been listening, 'I believe this one can.'
'Impossible!' cried the Emperor.
'It's mechanical,' the watchmaker explained, 'If I wind it up for you it'll sing a song.

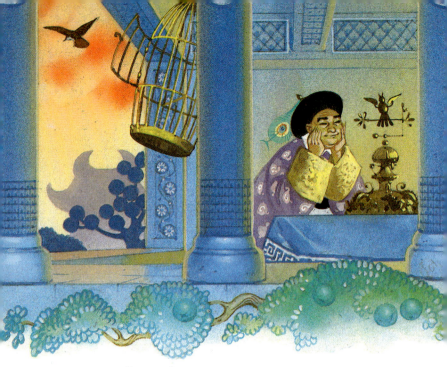

So while the Emperor looked on, the watchmaker carefully turned the key on the side of the golden bird. As soon as he had finished, the golden perch slowly began to bounce up and down and the little bird started to turn around and around on the perch and dance.

'What a strange and beautiful creature,' the Emperor laughed. As he spoke, the little golden bird lifted its head and began to sing.

The song that came out of its mouth was as beautiful as the nightingale's song. The Emperor listened and listened, and soon there were tears in his eyes.

'Aaah,' whispered the Emperor to his mechanical bird, 'now you're my greatest treasure. You're the more valuable bird because you can never fly away and leave me.'

The little nightingale heard what the Emperor said to the golden bird.

'The Emperor is happy now. He does not need me,' the nightingale thought to itself.

The nightingale was right because when it flew out of its cage and into the night, the Emperor did not even notice that it had gone. And when the nightingale sang its song in the forest that night, the Emperor did not hear it.

Every morning, every afternoon, every evening, and every night, the watchmaker came and wound up the golden bird for the Emperor.

Now it was the music of the golden bird that surrounded the Emperor everywhere he went. He loved his mechanical bird so much that he forgot all about the nightingale.

One morning, the watchmaker wound up the mechanical bird as usual. However, this time it did not bounce, it did not turn around, it did not dance and it did not sing. Instead, it went Brrrrr, then Bzzzz, and then it fell off its little perch onto the floor.

'My golden bird!' cried the Emperor, 'my greatest treasure! What's happened to it? It's your fault,' he said to the watchmaker. 'You've broken my bird, and if you don't mend it soon, you'll be sorry!'

The watchmaker worked for hours and hours, trying to mend the little golden bird. Finally, it began to sing again, but its song was weak and slow. The watchmaker told the Emperor that the bird was growing tired and old.

'If you make this bird sing more than once a year,' he said, 'it'll break and I won't be able to mend it.'

The Emperor thought for a few moments and then sadly agreed with the watchmaker. The golden bird was allowed to sing only once a year, on the Emperor's birthday.

While the Emperor waited for his birthday, he thought about the other nightingale. He sent his men into the forest, and they looked and looked, and listened very carefully, but the nightingale had disappeared.

The Emperor had no music in his life now and he hated peace and quiet. But he did not want to listen to his old musicians, he only wanted to hear the nightingale's song.

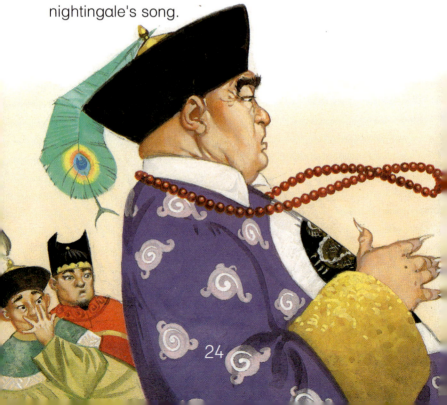

One day, he called the watchmaker.

'Bring me the mechanical bird this very minute,' he said.

'But, your Majesty,' said the watchmaker, 'it's not your birthday.'

'Bring it to me now!' shouted the Emperor, and he was so angry that the watchmaker was afraid. So he brought the mechanical bird and he slowly began to wind it up.

'Ahh, my treasure,' said the Emperor as the bird began to sing, but then it suddenly stopped singing and made the most awful noise: zing, tring, bing kerdoing!

The Emperor covered his eyes, and when he looked, he saw that his golden bird had broken into a hundred pieces.

The Emperor went to bed and stayed there for two whole weeks. His men tried to wake him up, but he would not open his eyes. They brought him his favourite food, but he would not eat it. They sat by his bed and told him their funniest jokes, but he did not laugh at them. The finest musicians in the country came to play to him, but he did not respond to their music. Everybody thought that the Emperor was going to die.

'It's never been so quiet here,' they whispered.

The Emperor lay on his bed, tired and weak, his eyes closed. It was midnight, all was quiet and everyone was asleep but him. Suddenly, his room was full of the most beautiful music.

'I must be dreaming,' thought the Emperor, because I can hear the sweetest voice in the world. I can hear the voice of my little nightingale.'

And he was right. The nightingale was sitting on a tree outside the Emperor's window and it sang its sweet song to the Emperor all night long. Soon the Emperor fell into a deep sleep.

When the Emperor woke up the next morning, he had a big smile on his face. His men raced into the room to see him. He sat up in bed and opened his eyes wide. He gave a big yawn, a big stretch and ordered a big breakfast.

'Bring me enough food for twenty men!' he said, licking his lips.

'Oh, and prepare the great hall,' he smiled, 'because this evening there'll be a huge festival. I want you to clean that hall from floor to ceiling ... I want a thousand lanterns and a golden perch ...'

The Emperor's men laughed and started to prepare the great hall for the festival.

That evening, like the evening long before, the nightingale flew in through the window, sat on its golden perch, and sang its strange and beautiful song. When it had finished, the Emperor had tears in his eyes.

'Thank you, little bird,' he smiled.

This time the Emperor did not give the nightingale a golden cage and he did not ask it to stay. The Emperor's guests were very surprised when the little nightingale flew out through the window and went back into the forest.

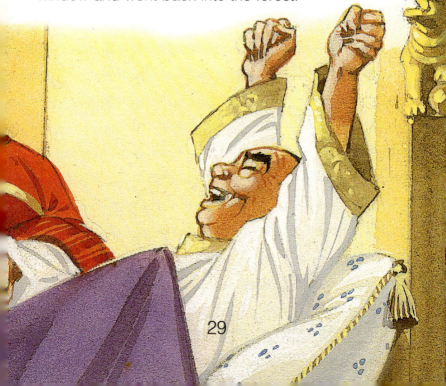

However, that night when everyone was asleep the little nightingale returned to the palace. It sat in the trees outside the Emperor's window and sang its sweet, strange and beautiful song.

This time, the Emperor did not tell anyone about the nightingale. It was their secret. The Emperor laughed when he remembered the mechanical bird.

'O, Nightingale,' he whispered, 'you are more valuable than any gold or diamonds. You are truly my greatest treasure.'

Every night after that, the little nightingale returned to the Emperor's window to send him gently to sleep with its song.

Activities

Before you read

1. There are two birds in 'The Emperor and the Nightingale'.

a  b

Describe the difference between bird 'a' and bird 'b' in three sentences.

_____
_____
_____

2. Look at the picture below. Can you describe what is happening?

After you read

I. Below, there are twelve hidden words. Can you find them?

P	E	R	C	H	B	G	L	R	D
E	V	A	L	U	A	B	L	E	Z
M	P	E	A	C	E	F	U	L	C
P	O	W	E	R	F	U	L	S	H
E	G	O	L	D	E	N	A	M	I
R	E	D	S	P	O	N	N	G	N
O	T	M	A	J	E	S	T	Y	A
R	F	R	T	K	S	T	E	A	R
W	F	H	U	Q	E	M	R	U	P
J	E	W	E	L	S	D	N	E	T

2. 'You are more valuable than any gold or diamonds,' the Emperor said to the nightingale at the end of the story.
What does it mean? What lesson did the Emperor learn?